Original title:
Wool and Winter Winds

Copyright © 2024 Creative Arts Management OÜ
All rights reserved.

Author: Julian Montgomery
ISBN HARDBACK: 978-9916-94-420-2
ISBN PAPERBACK: 978-9916-94-421-9

Ghostly Whispers of Warmth

In the quiet night, shadows creep,
Echoes of laughter, secrets to keep.
Fleeting moments, soft as a sigh,
Ghostly whispers float, like dreams passing by.

Memories linger, wrapped in the haze,
Warmth of their presence, a comforting blaze.
Haunting and gentle, they call out my name,
In this dance of time, nothing feels the same.

Stars weave stories in the silk of the dark,
Flickering softly, each luminous spark.
The air hums softly, with tales of the past,
Ghostly whispers of warmth, forever they'll last.

Close to the heart, where shadows unite,
Guided by whispers, they flicker with light.
Fading yet bright, like a love that remains,
Ghostly whispers of warmth, easing the pains.

Embracing Solace in the Frost

Silent whispers fill the air,
Gentle flakes of snow descend.
In the stillness, burdens bare,
Frozen moments, time to mend.

Footprints trace a path unique,
Nature's canvas, pure and bright.
In the frost, my heart can speak,
Finding peace within the white.

Twisted Fibers of Memory

Threads of time weave through my mind,
Colors fade, yet stories stay.
In the tapestry, love aligned,
Moments cherished in the fray.

Each strand holds a gentle light,
Echoes of a laughter shared.
In the shadows, warmth ignites,
Twisted fibers, love declared.

The Handwoven Heart

Woven tightly, hearts combine,
Each detail tells a tale anew.
In the fabric, love's design,
Threads of hope and trust imbue.

Every stitch a promise made,
Soft caress through trial's test.
In this craft, my fears do fade,
Handwoven heart, forever blessed.

Chilly Air and Harvest Fires

As the daylight softly wanes,
Chilly air begins to creep.
In the fields, the harvest gains,
Flames that warm, as shadows leap.

Embers crackle, night unfolds,
Stories shared under starlight.
In the warmth, a love retold,
Chilly air and fires bright.

Soft Threads of Solitude

In quiet corners, whispers play,
Where shadows dance in shades of gray.
A fragile peace finds room to breathe,
Soft threads of solitude we weave.

Among the walls that hold our dreams,
The mind unravels, or so it seems.
With every thought, a silent flight,
In soft cocoon, we embrace the night.

Each moment lingers, sweet and shy,
Like fleeting clouds that drift on high.
Through empty halls, a soft refrain,
Threads of solitude, a gentle chain.

Whispered Chills of the Night

The moon hangs high, a silver eye,
Casting whispers, a soft sigh.
In shadows deep, secrets unfold,
Chills of the night, quiet yet bold.

Winds caress with a haunting tune,
Legendary tales, beneath the moon.
Each rustling leaf, a story told,
In whispered chills, the night grows cold.

Stars twinkle like distant eyes,
Guardians lost in velvet skies.
As dreams take flight on gossamer wings,
The night reveals what silence brings.

Knit of the Frosted Dawn

Morning breaks with a tender light,
The world adorned in frosted white.
Each blade of grass, a crystal lace,
In knit of dawn, we find our place.

Birds awaken, sweet songs in air,
Nature's chorus, beyond compare.
The sun peeks through with golden ray,
Warming hearts as night doth sway.

A chilly breath on skin does flow,
Hints of winter in gentle glow.
With every step, the earth takes hold,
In knit of dawn, a story told.

Sanctuary in the Storm

When thunder rolls and shadows loom,
In tempest's heart, we find our room.
The world outside, a wild spree,
Yet in this space, we feel so free.

Raindrops tap a rhythmic song,
A lullaby where we belong.
Together here, through every plight,
A sanctuary in the stormy night.

The fire crackles, warmth and light,
While outside rages nature's might.
We hold each other, fears aside,
In storm's embrace, forever tied.

Texture of Quietude

In the stillness, whispers weave,
Softly draping the evening's sleeve.
A gentle hush, the world retreats,
As time slows down, and calmness greets.

In shadows deep, secrets unfold,
Wrapped in warmth, like threads of gold.
Fingers trace the air so light,
In this space, all feels just right.

Hearts find solace in the night,
Where dreams take wing, in silent flight.
The fabric of peace, tightly wrought,
In the quietude, solace is sought.

Veil of the Blustery Night

Underneath a canvas of stars,
A tapestry of dreams and scars.
The wind howls soft, a haunting sound,
A shroud of secrets wrapped around.

Branches sway like dancers bold,
In this night's embrace, stories told.
Whispers of life, both fierce and free,
Under the veil, all things can be.

Moonlight flickers, casting its glow,
On paths unknown, where no one goes.
With every gust, the heart ignites,
In the veil of the blustery nights.

Threads of Resilience

In the fabric of time, we find our place,
Woven with strength, an unyielding grace.
Each strand tells tales of trials faced,
A tapestry rich, never erased.

When storms arise and shadows claim,
We stand together, calling our name.
With threads of courage, we stitch anew,
A legacy bright, a bond so true.

Through every fracture, beauty grows,
In resilience, the heart bestows.
A quilt of dreams, with love we weave,
In every stitch, together we believe.

Nestled in Gales

In the eye of the storm, we find our breath,
Amidst howling winds, and whispers of death.
With a heart of flame, we stand so tall,
Embraced by gales, we will not fall.

The tempest rages, but here we bloom,
In chaos' dance, we chase the gloom.
Roots sink deep, through earth and stone,
In the wild winds, we find our home.

For in every gust, we find our song,
A melody fierce, where we belong.
Nestled in gales, we learn to soar,
With spirits free, we crave for more.

Scenes of Softness

Gentle whispers in the night,
Moonlight dances, pure and bright.
Canvas painted, hues so mild,
Nature's cradle, soft and wild.

Petals drop on velvet grass,
Moments fleeting, yet they pass.
Every shadow, every gleam,
Frames of life, a tender dream.

Breath of the Frosted Field

Morning rises, crisp and clear,
Softly sighs the winter's cheer.
Blankets of white, a quiet shroud,
Silent whispers, nature proud.

Footprints linger on the ground,
In this stillness, peace is found.
Every breath, a cloud of mist,
Frosty kisses, nature's tryst.

Sable and Thread

In the twilight, shadows weave,
Threads of darkness, dreams believe.
Colors blend in twilight's glow,
Stories whispered, soft and slow.

Midnight's fabric, rich and deep,
Holding secrets that we keep.
Stitch by stitch, the night unfolds,
Tales of wonder, tales of old.

Caressing the Chill

Breeze that dances through the trees,
Bringing whispers, sweet and free.
Frosty breath upon my skin,
Nature's touch, where warmth begins.

Every leaf in winter's hold,
Wonders wrapped in shimmered cold.
Moments shared with sky and earth,
In this chill, I find my worth.

Dreaming in Layers

Whispers of twilight gently unfold,
Beneath the starlit sky, dreams take hold.
Layers of wishes, wrapped in the night,
Softly they shimmer, bathed in soft light.

A tapestry woven of hopes and despair,
Colors of twilight dance in the air.
Each thread a moment, each knot a chance,
In the realm of slumber, we whimsically prance.

The echoes of memories, floating like fog,
Filling the spaces where shadows may log.
In this soft haven, where time gently bends,
The heart finds solace, as dreaming transcends.

Fabric of the Night

Stars are stitched in a cloak of dark blue,
A silken embrace where the moonlight breaks through.
Threads of silence weave a delicate dream,
In the fabric of night, nothing's as it seems.

Each twinkle a secret, old stories retold,
In whispers of twilight, their magic unfolds.
Bathed in the glow of celestial glee,
The night wraps around, cradling softly.

Winds carry tales from forgotten places,
While shadows dance slowly, revealing their faces.
In the stillness, hearts open wide,
In the fabric of night, we easily hide.

Breaths of the Distant Hearth

From far echoes of warmth, a fire still glows,
Its whispering flames tell tales that it knows.
Breaths of the distant hearth beckon us near,
To feel their embrace, to hold them so dear.

Ashes of memories, softly they rise,
Carried aloft by the wind to the skies.
The crackle of woodness sings sweet lullabies,
In the glow of the warmth, our worries subside.

Bringing forth comfort, a flickering light,
Guiding our journeys through the veil of the night.
In moments of stillness, we gather as one,
Around the warm hearth, where battles are won.

Muffled Murmurs

Within the quiet, soft whispers arise,
Muffled murmurs sway, as shadows disguise.
Secrets entangled in the depths of the night,
Flickering thoughts concealed from our sight.

Every sigh carries a flicker of dreams,
Drifting like clouds over moonlit streams.
Voices in echoes, softly they weave,
Stories untold, waiting to believe.

In the stillness, the heart learns to listen,
To the gentle hush where the stars glisten.
Muffled murmurs cradle the soul with delight,
In the quiet embrace of the soothing night.

Memory of Fire and Fabric

In the hearth, the flames dance bright,
Threads of stories weave through the night.
Echoed laughter fills the air,
Warmth surrounds, a bond we share.

Faded blankets and worn-out seams,
Hold the whispers of our dreams.
Each ember glows with tales untold,
Memories wrapped in a blanket of gold.

Sparks rise up like fleeting thoughts,
Captured in the waves of knots.
The flickering light guides our way,
In the tapestry of yesterday.

Time pauses as shadows delight,
In the memory of fire, we hold tight.
Fabric of moments, stitched with grace,
In the warmth of love, we find our place.

Cold-Weather Lullabies

The wind whispers soft lullabies,
Beneath the gray of winter skies.
Snowflakes dance in the frosty air,
A silent kiss, a gentle care.

Fires crackle, shadows play,
As night takes hold, and dreams sway.
Blankets snug against the chill,
In hushed tones, the world stands still.

Footsteps muffled on the street,
Children giggle where rooftops meet.
A warm embrace, cocoa in hand,
In cozy corners, we understand.

Stars twinkle like distant dreams,
In the quiet, hope redeems.
Cold-weather lullabies remind,
Of warmth and love, so intertwined.

Whirlwinds of Comfort

In the tempest, we find our way,
Holding close what words can't say.
Whirlwinds spin with tender might,
Guiding souls through darkest night.

Where chaos reigns and fears collide,
Love becomes the shining guide.
In the storm, we brace and bend,
Finding strength in hearts that mend.

Through swirling winds, laughter flows,
A balm for wounds that life bestows.
We gather close, an anchored fleet,
In whirlwinds of comfort, we find our seat.

Hand in hand, we face the gale,
Stories woven as we prevail.
Together, we rise and claim our right,
To dance again in the soft moonlight.

Shelter in the Storm

When clouds gather and winds do wail,
We seek shelter, a heart's prevail.
A haven found in arms so warm,
Together we weather the fierce storm.

Raindrops tap on windows tight,
Creating a symphony of night.
In the chaos, a calm emerges,
As love's light within us surges.

Stories shared like flickering flames,
Unraveling fears, calling names.
In the tempest, we are reborn,
Finding solace in hearts that are worn.

So let the raging storms resume,
We have each other, we clear the gloom.
In every thunder, and every tear,
We'll stand united, dispelling fear.

Tapestry of Frost

Winter whispers softly, as the world turns white,
Each flake a gentle story, in the pale moonlight.
Branches wear crystal gowns, twinkling in the air,
Nature weaves its magic, with intricate care.

The silent nights are painted, with a frosty brush,
Underneath the starlit sky, there's a calming hush.
Footprints in the powder, a tale yet untold,
In the tapestry of frost, secrets to unfold.

Morning dew glimmers, on grasses bowing low,
A silent serenade, in the dawn's soft glow.
Each breath we see hovering, in the chilly breeze,
Winter's art unfolds gently, with perfect ease.

As chilly winds awaken, the world starts to sigh,
Beneath the frosted canopy, dreams begin to fly.
Patterns shift and shimmer, in this quiet land,
A tapestry of frost, crafted by nature's hand.

Cozy Shadows

In the corner of the room, where whispers softly blend,
A cocoon of cozy shadows, where the day can end.
Blankets wrapped in warmth, like a gentle embrace,
Time slows in the soft light, in this sacred space.

Flickering candle flames, dance in playful arcs,
Illuminating laughter, revealing hidden sparks.
Outside the world may hurry, but here we find our rest,
In the heart of cozy shadows, we feel truly blessed.

The smell of spiced cider, wafts through the air,
While stories weave together, a tapestry rare.
With every heartfelt moment, memories are spun,
In cozy shadows gathered, we find peace as one.

As twilight softly blankets, the world in deep blue,
We nestle in the warmth, with the ones we hold true.
Safe from every storm, in this small, cherished nook,
Cozy shadows cradle, the love that we took.

Threads of the Season

Golden leaves are falling, swirling in the breeze,
Nature's quilt of colors, rustling through the trees.
Each thread tells a story, of warmth and of cheer,
As autumn's gentle touch, brings the harvest near.

The air smells of apple, cinnamon, and spice,
Gathered 'round the table, where we share our lives.
With laughter and with joy, we weave our dreams tight,
Threads of the season spinning, in the fading light.

Crisp mornings awaken, with a painted sky low,
Footsteps crunch on the path, where the wildflowers grow.
In every loving gesture, in every sweet sound,
We find the threads of season, in the love that surrounds.

As twilight wraps the day, in a quilted embrace,
We cherish every moment, each smile on a face.
For in the threads of season, we find our true place,
A tapestry of memories, time cannot erase.

Gossamer Frost

Dawn breaks with a shimmer, on the window's pane,
Gossamer frost whispers, in a delicate chain.
Nature's breath suspended, like a dream out of reach,
Every crystal a lesson, that silence can teach.

Softly it blankets the world in a light embrace,
Turning fields into canvas, a magical space.
Laughter fills the air, as children play outside,
In gossamer frost's beauty, where winter's dreams hide.

Each morning brings a promise, of wonder anew,
With every breath we take, in the frosty blue.
Wings of frost caress, the edges of our mind,
Gossamer tales unfold, in this magic we find.

As daylight slowly warms, the frost begins to fade,
Yet the memories linger, in the dance that we've made.
So we hold onto moments, like treasures we keep,
In gossamer frost's memory, our hearts softly leap.

Celestial Fibers

Threads of starlight weave the night,
Glistening softly, pure and bright.
Winds of whispers spin and dance,
In this vast cosmic expanse.

Nebulas bloom like flowers rare,
In the fabric of the air.
Galaxies swirl, a wondrous sight,
Stitched with dreams, they take to flight.

Constellations draw their lines,
Mapping secrets, ancient signs.
In the loom of time and space,
Every star finds its own place.

Infinity in every seam,
Woven whispers, cosmic dream.
In this tapestry we share,
Celestial fibers, light as air.

Snug Beneath the Stars

Wrapped in blankets, warm and tight,
Underneath the velvet night.
Stars above begin to gleam,
Cradling hopes like a sweet dream.

The moon whispers soft and low,
Guiding wishes as they flow.
Crickets sing their lullabies,
As the world in slumber lies.

Fires crackle, embers glow,
Painting shadows, soft and slow.
In this moment, time stands still,
Hearts are hushed, the world fulfills.

Snug beneath the endless skies,
Wrapped in warmth, where magic lies.
Holding tight to fleeting hours,
Under stars, we bloom like flowers.

Enveloping Chill

Winter's breath, a crisp caress,
Nipping gently, nothing less.
Frosty whispers, quiet night,
Nature's cloak, a shimm'ring sight.

Trees stand bare, their branches sigh,
Blanketed 'neath a slate-gray sky.
Footsteps crunch on sparkling snow,
As the world begins to glow.

Shivers dance along the skin,
A reminder that warmth is kin.
Yet in this chill, life finds a spark,
In the stillness, whispers hark.

Enveloping, the season calls,
Nature's beauty enthralls.
In the silent, starlit chill,
Winter's magic lingers still.

Fleece and Firelight

Fleece wraps round in cozy twine,
Crackling flames, a heartbeat sign.
Stories shared, laughter bright,
In the warm embrace of light.

Shadows play upon the walls,
Echoing each tale that falls.
Outside the dark, the world sleeps deep,
While inside, memories we keep.

Sipping cocoa, hearts unwind,
In the glow, we are entwined.
Fireside glimmers, soft and clear,
Binding moments we hold dear.

Fleece and firelight, our retreat,
A sanctuary, warm and sweet.
In this haven, time stands still,
With every breath, we drink our fill.

Patterns in the Snow

Footprints trace the winter's dance,
Swirling in a fleeting glance.
Each print tells a secret tale,
Of fleeting moments, soft and pale.

Branches bow with frosty grace,
Nature's quilt in white embrace.
Silent whispers all around,
In this canvas, peace is found.

Rays of sun through clouds will slip,
Casting shadows, winter's grip.
Footsteps lead to places new,
Where frosty dreams come into view.

Patterns weave a story bright,
In the heart of winter's night.
Each snowflake, unique and pure,
A masterpiece that will endure.

Tucked Away in Warmth

Cocooned in blankets, snug and tight,
Fireside crackles, warmth ignites.
Outside, the world is cold and gray,
Inside, love glows in soft array.

Tea is brewed, its steam does rise,
Comfort found in cozy sighs.
With every page of books we read,
Hearts entwined, we plant the seed.

Laughter dances in the air,
Joyful moments, free from care.
Time slows down within these walls,
As winter sings its icy calls.

Tucked away from stormy nights,
Building dreams with flickering lights.
Together, we find we are strong,
In this warmth, we both belong.

Embracing the Icy Breath

Cold winds whisper through the trees,
Nature's breath, a chill that frees.
Each inhalation, sharp and clear,
Embracing winter, year by year.

Frosty air caresses skin,
A dance begins, where dreams can spin.
Each chill ignites the soul's delight,
As stars emerge in velvet night.

We tread softly on the frost,
In a world of beauty lost.
With every step, the echoes sing,
Of winter's grace and all it brings.

In this art of cold and calm,
We find our peace, a soothing balm.
Embracing every icy breath,
There's magic found in winter's depth.

Hearthbound Whispers

Fires crackle, shadows dance,
Warmth surrounds in soft expanse.
Voices blend in gentle tone,
In this haven, we are home.

Stories flow like river's song,
Binding us, we all belong.
Muffled laughter, time suspended,
In these moments, hearts are tended.

Glimmers of light, soft and low,
Illuminating tales of old.
Each whisper carries love's intent,
In the hearth where time is spent.

Hearthbound whispers, secrets shared,
In this warmth, we are prepared.
Through the night, we'll hold on tight,
Together wrapped in love's pure light.

Snow-Kissed Textiles

Blankets draped on frosty days,
Threads of warmth in winter's gaze.
Colors bright against the white,
Woven dreams in soft twilight.

Looms whisper tales of old,
Patterns rich like stories told.
In each stitch, a memory spins,
Wrapped in love where comfort begins.

Flakes of snow fall from the sky,
Covering all as they drift by.
Textures dance in chilly glee,
Nature's touch, a tapestry.

With every layer, hearts entwine,
Crafted pieces, pure and fine.
Snow-kissed textiles warmly share,
The essence of this season's care.

Yarn of the North

From distant lands where cold winds blow,
Yarn is spun with a gentle flow.
Colorful strands of stories bright,
Crafted by hands, a pure delight.

Frosted evenings, fires glow,
Knitting dreams in soft tableau.
Each loop a journey, each twist a turn,
Lessons of warmth and love we learn.

Wool from sheep that graze the plain,
Soft as whispers, gentle as rain.
Threads connect us, strong and warm,
Woven tightly through every storm.

Yarn of the North holds us near,
In its embrace, we shed our fear.
Through every stitch, hope can grow,
Creating comfort from the frosty flow.

Hearthside Comforts

Crackling flames and shadows play,
Hearthside comforts end the day.
Warmth surrounds, a gentle hug,
In every corner, cozy snug.

Tea infused with fragrant spice,
Fingers wrapped 'round mugs of nice.
Double-knitted against the chill,
Every sip, a warmth to fill.

Throw blankets piled high and neat,
Gentle laughter, friends to greet.
Moments cherished, hearts align,
In this space, the world feels fine.

As the seasons sway and shift,
Hearthside comforts are the gift.
Holding close what matters most,
In this glow, we share a toast.

Breezes Through the Loom

Breezes whisper through the loom,
Nature's gifts in every room.
A tapestry of gentle light,
Weaving dreams both day and night.

Threads of green and skies of blue,
Each creation feels so true.
With every stitch, the story flows,
In the fabric, life bestows.

Sunshine dances on the threads,
Crimson poppies grace the beds.
Hands of craft create a bond,
In this world, we dream beyond.

Breezes through the loom invite,
Artisan hearts to share their light.
Creating beauty, pure embrace,
A woven tapestry of grace.

Chills in the Air

A rustle in the trees, soft sighs,
The frost nips gently, winter tries.
With breath like smoke, we tread the night,
The world aglow, beneath moonlight.

Echoes of silence, crisp and clear,
Whispers of winter draw us near.
Each step leaves shadows, swift and swift,
In the chill, a hidden gift.

Biting winds, they wrap around,
Nature's shiver, a haunting sound.
In the distance, a hoot, a call,
The chill enfolds, embracing all.

Hearts beat wild in the freezing air,
In every exhale, memories flare.
Wrapped in warmth like a tender prayer,
Together, we breathe—chills in the air.

Whispering Fibers

Threads of twilight, woven tight,
Tales of warmth in the fading light.
Whispers dance on gentle seams,
Promises stitched in silken dreams.

Fingers trace the fabric's grace,
Each loop and knot, a soft embrace.
In every color, stories swirl,
A tapestry of love unfurl.

The loom hums sweet with every breath,
Crafting comfort, defying death.
As shadows lengthen, night grows near,
Those whispered fibers hold us dear.

In cosy corners, wrapped and warm,
We find our peace, away from harm.
Though storms may come and chill the land,
Within these threads, forever stand.

Soft Embrace of Cold

Gentle flakes fall from the sky,
Each one a whisper, a muted sigh.
The world transforms in pale white veils,
Nature's breath, where silence prevails.

In the quiet hush, we lose our way,
Snowflakes dance, inviting play.
Hand in hand, we wander far,
Guided by winter's silver star.

The crispness bites with a playful tease,
As we curl up beneath the trees.
With steaming cups, we warm our souls,
In the cold, our laughter rolls.

Soft embrace, a chilling trend,
Fires crackle, warmth to send.
In winter's grip, love does unfold,
In every heartbeat, soft and cold.

Stitches Beneath the Snow

Beneath the blanket, quiet lies,
A winter hush, beneath the skies.
Stitches weave the earth's defense,
Holding secrets, building sense.

Under frost, the roots still dream,
Nature's pulse, a silent stream.
Every flake, a tale untold,
Binds the past and future bold.

In the soft white cradle, life awaits,
Gathering strength, as it creates.
Each stitch, a promise to renew,
In the quiet, hope shines through.

When spring arrives, a vibrant show,
Revealing the stitches 'neath the snow.
In warmth we'll find what winter sews,
Life's tapestry, as garden grows.

Cozy Embrace of the Hearth

In the glow of amber light,
We gather close, hearts alight.
Whispers dance on gentle breeze,
Wrapped in warmth, our souls find ease.

Crackling logs, a soothing sound,
Flickering flames, joy profound.
Stories shared in soft delight,
In this haven, love takes flight.

The chill outside, a distant song,
Inside these walls, we all belong.
With every sip of cocoa sweet,
Life's simple moments make us complete.

So let the world turn cold and gray,
Here in this space, we choose to stay.
Bound by warmth, forever near,
In cozy embrace, we conquer fear.

Shivering Shadows and Warmth

Shadows flicker, edges blur,
Outside the window, winds do stir.
A world of frost, a tale untold,
Yet here we sit, defying the cold.

Under blankets, snug and tight,
Our laughter echoes, pure delight.
Fireside chats and whispered dreams,
Creating warmth from winter's schemes.

Candles cast their soft embrace,
While hearts collide in gentle grace.
Each moment shared, a treasure kept,
In shivering shadows, we have leapt.

With every breath, the chill retreats,
As love blooms warm in simple feats.
Together we find solace, true,
In shivering shadows, me and you.

The Comfort of Thrifted Dreams

In dusty shops where treasures lie,
We sift through memories, you and I.
Each thrifted gem, a tale to tell,
In faded prints, our hearts do dwell.

A porcelain cup, a quilt that's frayed,
In these small things, time's magic played.
We breathe life into what was lost,
Finding joy despite the cost.

The laughter shared in cozy nooks,
Among the pages of old books.
Each dream we seek, a thread that's spun,
In thrifted trinkets, we have won.

With every find, our spirits soar,
In worn-out spaces, we adore.
The comfort found in simple schemes,
Awakens in us thrifted dreams.

Frosty Breath of Silent Days

Morning light breaks through the haze,
Chasing shadows of frosty days.
Each breath we take, a puff of white,
In winter's grip, we find our light.

Snowflakes twirl in dazzling flight,
Nature whispers, pure and bright.
With every step, a crunching sound,
In silent hours, peace is found.

Trees draped in their crystal coats,
On frozen lakes, the joy remote.
Yet in the quiet, hearts do sway,
In frosty breath of silent days.

So let us wander, hand in hand,
Through frosty fields, a winterland.
With chilly air, our spirits raise,
In frosty breath of silent days.

Spirit of the Snows

Whispers soft in frosty air,
The spirit dances, light and fair.
Snowflakes twirl in gentle flight,
Blanketing the world in white.

Footprints vanish, lost in time,
Silent secrets, pure sublime.
Nature's hush wraps all in grace,
Embracing winter's coldest face.

Beneath the pale and starry veil,
Stories hidden in each trail.
Winds of winter softly call,
Echoes linger, sweet and small.

In the warmth of fireside glow,
Hearts find peace where cold winds blow.
The spirit of the snows will guide,
Through the darkness, winter's stride.

Canvas of the Cold

A canvas stretched where chill prevails,
The painter's brush of icy trails.
Blue and white in strokes so bold,
Art of winter, fierce and cold.

Mountains draped in silent dreams,
Reflecting light in silver beams.
Every flake a masterpiece,
Frozen whispers never cease.

Branches wear the crystal sheen,
Nature's beauty, pure and keen.
Underneath the snowflakes' sway,
Hearts are warmed in soft display.

As night descends with quiet grace,
Stars emerge, a twinkling lace.
In this chill, our spirits soar,
On the canvas, forevermore.

Embraced by Shadows

In twilight's grasp, the shadows creep,
Silent whispers, secrets deep.
Nighttime cloaks the world in gray,
Embraced by shadows, dreams at play.

Moonlight dances on the ground,
In the stillness, peace is found.
Softly rustling leaves do sigh,
Underneath the starry sky.

Figures move in hiding places,
Faint reflections, ghostly traces.
Yet in the dark, there's sweet repose,
Embraced by shadows, calm and close.

In every heart, a flicker glows,
Guiding paths where no light shows.
Together in the quiet night,
We find our way through shadowed light.

Nest in the Night

A cozy nook where dreams reside,
Wrapped in warmth, the world outside.
Cloaked in stars, the sky so vast,
In this nest, the night holds fast.

The gentle hum of crickets sing,
Whispers soft, the night takes wing.
Each heartbeat matched with softest breath,
In this solace, we find depth.

Beneath the blanket of the dark,
Every flicker makes its mark.
Nests of comfort, love entwined,
In the night, our souls aligned.

As shadows blend and night grows still,
We find peace beneath the chill.
In dreams we fly, hearts take their flight,
Together here, our nest in night.

Fireside Serenade

The flames they dance and twirl,
Whispers of warmth unfurl.
Shadows play upon the wall,
In this moment, we feel small.

Crackling wood, a soulful sound,
In this haven, peace is found.
Stories shared and laughter bright,
Beneath the stars, we hold the night.

Embers glow like fleeting dreams,
In the quiet, gentle gleams.
As the cool breeze softly sighs,
We find comfort in each other's eyes.

Time stands still as hours pass,
In this circle, love's our glass.
Fireside warmth that lingers near,
Together, we cast off all fear.

Vows of the Night

Stars above, a shining choir,
Whispers of love, soft as fire.
Promises made beneath the moon,
Hearts entwined, a sacred tune.

In the shadows, secrets blend,
Hand in hand, we transcend.
Every vow, a fragrant rose,
As the twilight's beauty grows.

Drifting dreams in midnight's care,
With each heartbeat, silent prayer.
Together we shall dance and glide,
Forever true, hearts open wide.

The night is young, our spirits soar,
With every glance, we ask for more.
Underneath the velvet sky,
Our love will never say goodbye.

Cradle of the Fleece

In cozy nooks, the warmth resides,
A cradle soft where comfort hides.
Wrapped in wool, the world feels right,
Through gentle dreams we greet the night.

Laughter echoes, threads entwined,
In this woollen love, we're aligned.
Close your eyes, let worries fade,
In this safe place, memories made.

Outside, the storm begins to howl,
Inside, we share a knowing smile.
The fleece enfolds with tender care,
As time slips by, we feel it rare.

In every stitch, a story spun,
Within the warmth, we come undone.
Close in this cradle, hearts will meet,
In the fabric of love, we find our beat.

Soft Echoes of the Past

Whispers linger in the air,
Memories weaving without a care.
Footsteps echo down the lane,
In each still moment, joy and pain.

Old photographs in frames aglow,
Remind us of the seeds we sow.
Laughter shared beneath the sun,
In faded echoes, we are one.

Time may change, but love remains,
In every heart, the same refrains.
Softly, we reminisce and sigh,
For in these moments, we never die.

Through velvet nights and golden days,
We celebrate in countless ways.
For every memory that we hold,
Is a treasure richer than gold.

Tangles of Heart and Hearth

In the quiet corners, memories sway,
Voices of laughter linger in play.
Threads of affection weave ever tight,
Binding the heart with warmth and light.

Echoes of footsteps whisper and cling,
Songs of the past, in unison sing.
Fires of comfort crackle and glow,
In the embrace of love, we grow.

Beneath the roof where dreams intertwine,
Moments like shadows in soft sunshine.
Here in the hush, our spirits align,
Tangled together, your heart and mine.

Warmth Wrapped in Echoes

Beneath the stars, where silence calls,
Softly the night around us falls.
Words hang like lanterns, glowing bright,
Illuminating thoughts in the night.

The warmth of your voice, a soothing breeze,
Caressing my soul with tender ease.
Wrapped in the echoes of things unsaid,
Finding my solace in the dreams we thread.

Time gently sways, like leaves in the air,
Moments unspoken, a language rare.
In this embrace, the world disappears,
Only our hearts beat, devoid of fears.

Spun Tales of the Cold

Frost-kissed windows tell stories anew,
Whispers of winter, both old and true.
Shadows flicker in the pale moonlight,
As the fire crackles, chasing the night.

Snowflakes drift like memories lost,
In the chill, we find warmth at any cost.
Wrapped in blankets, we share our dreams,
In the stillness, nothing is as it seems.

Tales spun of courage, hope, and grace,
In the cold, we discover our place.
Through the storm, hand in hand we roam,
Finding our hearts forever at home.

Beneath the Glistening Veil

Under the night sky, stars softly gleam,
Wrap us in magic, like a vivid dream.
Veils of the cosmos, shimmering bright,
Holding our secrets in the pale light.

Each twinkle a promise, a wish long cast,
Binding our futures with threads from the past.
The universe hums a sweet lullaby,
Cradling our hearts as time passes by.

In this vast moment, we find our way,
Guided by starlight, night turns to day.
Beneath the veil, we stand side by side,
In the harmony found where dreams abide.

Hushed Echoes of the Chill

In the stillness, whispers freeze,
Where shadows dance among the trees.
Breath hangs like mist, a spectral glow,
In the quiet, only silence flows.

Moonlight drapes the world in white,
Stars blink softly in the night.
Footsteps crunch on frosty ground,
A melody of peace is found.

Branches bow under a crystal weight,
Nature rests, in slumber's state.
Each echo holds a secret tale,
Of winter's breath, both soft and pale.

The chill lingers, time stands still,
In hushed echoes, the heart will fill.
Embraced by night, a gentle sigh,
Under the vast, eternal sky.

Frayed Edges of the Season

Leaves flutter down, like whispered dreams,
Colors fade, unraveling seams.
A tapestry worn, with edges frayed,
Memories linger in the shade.

Autumn's breath, a fleeting sigh,
Clouded skies, as birds fly by.
Crimson and gold, a soft farewell,
Each gust carries a silent bell.

Time weaves tales of love and fear,
Moments woven, both far and near.
The chill hints at a coming freeze,
Nature's canvas, swaying with ease.

Harvest moon, a gentle glance,
In fading light, shadows dance.
The season's edges, frayed yet bright,
Crafting stories in the night.

Stitches of Silence Under Snow

Beneath the blanket, whispers fade,
Silent tales, carefully laid.
Snowflakes fall, a muted grace,
Softly stitching winter's face.

In stillness, shadows intertwine,
Nature's secret, pure and divine.
Branches adorned, in white attire,
Chill of night, a quiet fire.

Footprints vanish, lost in time,
Echoes silenced, in their prime.
Stitches holding dreams so close,
In a world that's wrapped in prose.

The night deepens, a shroud of calm,
Each breath exhaled, a healing balm.
Under snow, soft dreams drift slow,
In stitches of silence, where we grow.

The Threadbare Journey

Along the path, the colors fade,
Memories tangled, secrets laid.
Each step forward, a tale untold,
The threadbare journey, brave and bold.

Worn boots crunch on gravel's bite,
Chasing shadows, seeking light.
The road unwinds, a winding scroll,
In search of pieces to make one whole.

With every turn, new stories rise,
Beneath the vast, unclouded skies.
Yet through the wear, a beauty gleams,
In every stumble, a spark of dreams.

The journey stretches, both near and far,
Guided gently by the stars.
Threadbare memories, rich and sweet,
We weave our lives with every beat.

Frozen Cycles

In icy realms where silence breathes,
The world lies wrapped in winter's sheath.
Branches weave the frost's embrace,
Time stands still, in frozen space.

Shadows dance on crisp white ground,
Whispers drift without a sound.
Nature's breath, a frosty sigh,
Every heartbeat quick to die.

Echoes of a sun long gone,
Only night and snow to don.
The cycle turns, a slow refrain,
Yearning warmth, yet bound by pain.

Beneath the frost, life waits in dreams,
Holding tight to sunlit beams.
When the thaw begins to call,
The world will rise, and barriers fall.

The Craft of Warmth

In the hearth where shadows play,
The embers glow, in soft array.
Woolen threads and laughter blend,
With every stitch, the hours mend.

Chasing chills with tender light,
Hands entwined through winter's night.
Cocoa brewed with sweet delight,
Kindred spirits, hearts ignite.

Baking dreams in fragrant air,
Gifts of warmth, both light and care.
Every tale told, a soothing balm,
Healing hands that weave such calm.

In every room, the warmth we find,
A craft of love, by heart defined.
Through every winter, we will hold,
The stories whispered, warm and bold.

Looms of Solstice

In the stillness of the night,
Threads of silver, woven light.
Stars like lanterns in the dark,
Each a whispered, glowing spark.

Shadows stretch and softly sway,
Dancing light, the night's ballet.
On the loom of time, they weave,
Patterns of what we believe.

Sunrise waits, its colors blend,
The darkest hour meets its end.
Seasons spiral, intertwine,
In this dance, the sacred sign.

From the solstice, rebirth flows,
Life anew, as nature shows.
Weaving hopes in every thread,
As warmth returns, the cold will shed.

Frigid Nightfall

The stars emerge, a frosty treasure,
In winter's grasp, we find our measure.
Moonlight spills on blankets white,
Kissing softly, the frigid night.

Whispers glide on chilly air,
Boughs adorned with silver wear.
In quiet streets, the echoes play,
Dreams and shadows, drift away.

Fires crackle, stories thread,
Through the warmth, our spirits spread.
Yet outside, the world stands still,
Frigid nightfall, a tranquil chill.

While cold winds sing their lullaby,
In cozy nooks, we will not cry.
For in this night, together we're found,
As hearts ignite, no winter's bound.

Frosted Hues

In morning's gentle glow, we see,
A world wrapped soft in white decree.
Each branch adorned, a sparkling cheer,
Nature whispers, winter's here.

The breath of cold, so crisp and clear,
Paints landscapes far and near.
With every step, the crunch we hear,
A frosted dance, in silence, dear.

The skies a canvas, pale and blue,
As sunlight melts the frost anew.
A fleeting moment, pure and true,
Life in winter's frosted hues.

So let us cherish this serene,
As nature dons her frosted sheen.
In every flake, a dream we glean,
In winter's charm, forever keen.

Embers and Entwined Threads

In twilight's glow, the embers dance,
With flickering flames, a fiery romance.
Threads of warmth wrap around the night,
Whispers of stories in soft flickering light.

The shadows stretch, as laughter weaves,
Intertwined moments, our hearts believe.
Each spark a memory, bright and bold,
In the hearth of our love, secrets unfold.

Under the stars, we softly tread,
With every whisper, our hopes are fed.
Entwined as one, through joy and dread,
Together forever, on this thread we spread.

The embers glow, our spirits lift,
In the tapestry of life, love's greatest gift.
With every heartbeat, our souls entwine,
In this radiant warmth, forever shine.

The Quilted Atmosphere

Beneath a quilt of azure skies,
Nature's patchwork, a sweet surprise.
Fields of green, in vivid show,
Layered blooms, with colors flow.

The gentle breeze, a soft caress,
Embracing all in tenderness.
Clouds drifting by, in quiet song,
In this quilted world, we all belong.

Each mountain peak, each valley wide,
A stunning quilt, in nature's pride.
We roam the paths, with hearts so free,
In this vibrant quilt, just you and me.

As day gives way to crescent night,
Stars adorn the quilted light.
A tapestry of dreams conspire,
In this fine quilt, our hopes aspire.

Layered in Serenity

The morning sun breaks through the haze,
Soft golden light in gentle ways.
Layers of peace, like whispers shared,
In the stillness, our hearts laid bare.

The rustling leaves in tranquil air,
Each moment savored, free from care.
Flowing streams echo nature's song,
In this embrace, where we belong.

Mountains rise in majestic grace,
Nature's beauty, a sacred space.
With every breath, we find our ground,
Layered in serenity, love unbound.

As twilight looms, the stars ignite,
A canvas rich with dreams in sight.
In this stillness, we find our way,
Layered in peace, forever stay.

Patterns of the Chill

Whispers dance in frozen air,
Shadows weave without a care.
Nature's breath, a crystal song,
In the stillness, we belong.

Footprints traced on icy ground,
Secrets in the silence found.
Brittle branches, pale and bare,
Patterns form, a frosty flair.

Snowflakes twirl like fleeting dreams,
Glittering under moonlit beams.
Each pattern tells a tale unique,
In winter's fold, a voice so bleak.

As the cold envelops night,
Hearts ablaze with warmth and light.
In this chill, we grow as one,
Patterns shift, the day is done.

Stitched in Silence

Threads of stories intertwine,
Words unspoken, still we shine.
Every stitch, a memory bound,
In the quiet, love is found.

Tapestries of feelings sewn,
Underneath, our truth is grown.
Stitched together, hearts entwined,
In this silence, we are kind.

Threads of gold and shades of blue,
Weave our trust, both strong and true.
Each tight-knit bond, a sacred peace,
In the calm, our worries cease.

In the fabric of our days,
Silence speaks in gentle ways.
Every whisper, soft and clear,
Stitched in silence, love draws near.

The Comforting Cloak

Wrapped in warmth, a soft embrace,
The comforting cloak, our sacred space.
Threads of comfort, woven tight,
Shielding souls from the cold of night.

Each layer whispers tales of old,
In its folds, secrets unfold.
A gentle touch, a quiet grace,
In this cloak, a cherished place.

Through storms that howl and winds that bite,
This garment holds our dreams tonight.
A tapestry of love and care,
In its refuge, we breathe air.

Let the world outside be stark,
Within this cloak, we find a spark.
Together wrapped, hearts intertwined,
The comforting cloak, our peace defined.

Beneath a Shroud of Frost

Morning breaks with icy breath,
Nature draped in shrouded death.
Frosty veils on windows cling,
In this hush, the chill does sing.

Whispers drift on morning light,
Underneath, the world feels bright.
Frozen blooms, a still display,
Each petal kissed by winter's sway.

Beneath the frost, a pulse remains,
Life awaits when spring regains.
Silent promises in the cold,
Stories of the brave and bold.

While the world seems hushed and shy,
Hope lies waiting, not to die.
Beneath the shroud, a fire glows,
In frost's embrace, true love still flows.

Shadows of the Loomed Night

In the depths of quiet dark,
Whispers dance like fireflies,
Silent tales the moon imparts,
As the world beneath it sighs.

Fingers trace upon the air,
Secrets held in shadows' bend,
Lingering in weighted stares,
Time, it seems, begins to mend.

Stars are woven in the night,
Patterned dreams take flight and soar,
On the loom of fading light,
Craving just a little more.

Darkness holds a tender space,
Where the heart learns how to feel,
In the night's soft, warm embrace,
Every shadow becomes real.

Fables Woven in Indigo

In the threads of twilight hue,
Stories linger in the air,
Indigo whispers, old yet new,
Fabric of a dreamer's prayer.

Stitched with notions of the past,
Every point a tale untold,
Binding truths in shadows cast,
Fables shimmer, bright and bold.

With each wrap, a life unfolds,
Kaleidoscope of vivid grace,
Every stitch a heart that holds,
Love and loss in time and space.

Woven gently, night unfolds,
In these fibers dreams entwine,
Magic in these tales retold,
In the dark, the stars align.

Riddles of the Clouded Sky

Veils of gray in twilight's sigh,
Secrets linger, lost in dreams,
Every cloud, a question high,
Mysteries tangled in moonbeams.

Shifting shapes that hide and seek,
Voices echo in the wind,
Riddles softly start to speak,
As the evening's light rescinds.

In the folds of every shroud,
Hope and doubt collide in flight,
Stories hidden in the cloud,
Await the dawn to bring the light.

Crackling whispers call our name,
Nature's breath, a gentle sigh,
In these riddles, hearts reclaim,
Dreams that stretch into the sky.

The Knitted Embrace of Longing

Yarns of thought entwined and spun,
In the quiet, soft and sweet,
Longing flows like threads undone,
Stitching hearts where moments meet.

Each loop a whisper in the night,
Each cast a hope, a tender prayer,
Knitting dreams beneath the light,
Woven close, a sacred layer.

The embrace of woven time,
Wraps around the aching soul,
In the fibers, love's pure rhyme,
Filling spaces, making whole.

As the needles click in tune,
Every heartbeat, every song,
In this warmth of afternoon,
Finds a place where we belong.

Echoes of the Hearth

Crackling flames dance in the night,
Warmth envelops, pure delight.
Stories shared in the golden glow,
Memories linger, hearts aglow.

Embers whisper of times long gone,
Comfort in silence, echoes strong.
The scent of pine fills the air,
Each heartbeat a treasured prayer.

Whispers of the Season's Past

Leaves in twilight, softly sigh,
Colors flicker, then wave goodbye.
Footsteps crunch on pathways old,
Secrets of autumn, dreams retold.

Frosty breath upon the glass,
Echoes of moments that swiftly pass.
Nature's palette, rich and vast,
In every shadow a note from the past.

Chasing the Charms of Chill

Frosted windows, a wintry cheer,
Whispers of snowflakes drawing near.
Sleds and laughter fill the air,
Joy in each moment, carefree flair.

Chimneys puffing, spices warm,
Life's sweet rhythm, a gentle charm.
Chasing sunsets, lit by the glow,
In every heartbeat, the winds still blow.

Shelter from the Storm

Raindrops patter, a soothing song,
In the shadows, we all belong.
Hearts united against the night,
Holding each other, arms held tight.

Outside, a tempest, wild and free,
Inside, whispers of harmony.
A fire crackles, stories unfold,
In warmth and comfort, we are bold.

Palette of the Frost

Whispers of white on a silent morn,
Painted with frost, a new day is born.
Crisp air flows through the sleeping trees,
Nature wraps all in its icy freeze.

Glistening paths under the pale sunlight,
Shimmering jewels in the soft twilight.
Every breath is a cloud in the chill,
A moment captured, time stands still.

Echoes of laughter in snow-laden parks,
Children at play, leaving joyful marks.
Snowflakes dance in a gentle embrace,
A world transformed, a magical place.

Under the glow of the silvery moon,
Winter's soft hum is a soothing tune.
In this palette where dreams intertwine,
Frost paints the world, serene and divine.

Frosty Wishes

A wish upon frost, so delicate, bright,
Carried by winds in the chill of the night.
Whispering secrets while stars softly gleam,
In the hush of the hour, we dare to dream.

Snowflakes like wishes descend from the sky,
Each one a promise, a silent sigh.
Frosted trees stand like guardians old,
Holding the dreams that we dare to be bold.

The world wears a blanket of sparkling grace,
Hope twinkles softly in every cold place.
With every heartbeat, let wishes take flight,
Through the frost-kissed air on this magical night.

In the stillness we find a profound peace,
Trust the frosty wishes; let each one cease.
For in their embrace, we shall find our way,
Guided by dreams until the break of day.

Tired Heartbeats

In the quiet, heartbeats softly sigh,
Echoes of longing as time drifts by.
Fading embers of warmth once aglow,
In the stillness of night, memories flow.

Wrapped in shadows, where hopes used to dance,
Fleeting whispers, a forgotten romance.
Time takes its toll on the fragile and worn,
Each beat a reminder of dreams overborne.

Yet in the silence, there's strength to be found,
Through tired heartbeats, life goes round.
Bearing the weight of each sorrow and song,
Finding the rhythm where we all belong.

Through weary days and unyielding nights,
Resilience glimmers from hidden delights.
And though we are tired, we still dream anew,
With every heartbeat, there's hope breaking through.

The Weaving of Solace

In twilight's embrace, the threads intertwine,
Weaving of solace, a tapestry fine.
Each moment a fiber, each sigh a new hue,
Crafting a vision as fresh as the dew.

The loom of our hearts holds stories untold,
A pattern of warmth in the depths of the cold.
Soft whispers of peace in the fabric of night,
Stitching together our fears and our light.

With each gentle thread, connection is made,
In the fabric of friendship, no bond shall fade.
Together we gather, our voices in song,
Weaving our solace where we all belong.

As time unfolds stories in numerous shades,
The weaving of solace never degrades.
For in every moment, we find what we seek,
The warmth of togetherness, tender and sleek.

Hearthside Whispers and Dreams

By the fire's gentle glow,
Soft whispers dance and flow.
Tales of love and warmth unfold,
In the night, a world of gold.

Embers crackle, shadows sway,
Memories drift like clouds in gray.
Silent wishes, hopes take flight,
In the heart, a spark ignites.

Fingers trace the stories spun,
Gathering dreams, one by one.
Each flicker holds a promise dear,
In the hearthside's embrace, we're near.

As the night wraps its tender cloak,
In the warmth, our spirits woke.
Together we weave in this space,
A tapestry of time and grace.

Warmth in the Frigid Air

Outside the world is cold and bare,
Yet we find our warmth with care.
Laughter lingers, hearts ignite,
Against the chill, we hold on tight.

Frosty breath in crystal streams,
Huddled close, we share our dreams.
Hands entwined, in laughter bright,
Together we chase the night.

Through the windows, winter glows,
Underneath the stars, love flows.
In the stillness, we hear the song,
A melody that keeps us strong.

With every chill that comes our way,
We find a reason still to stay.
In warmth, we find a shelter rare,
A home made strong in frigid air.

Knitted Dreams

With every stitch, a tale unfurls,
In yarn and thread, the beauty swirls.
Knitting memories, time entwined,
A tapestry of love defined.

Soft colors weave through gentle hands,
Creating warmth that understands.
In every loop, a wish concealed,
A knitted dream, our hearts revealed.

In cozy nooks, we sit at ease,
Crafting solace with love's decrees.
Each pattern tells of hope and grace,
In knitted dreams, we find our place.

As seasons change, and threads may fray,
These knitted dreams will still display.
In every fold, the warmth will bloom,
A cherished gift that fills the room.

Frosted Threads

Frosted threads on branches cling,
Winter's breath, a gentle sting.
In the stillness, beauty sighs,
Underneath the silver skies.

Each frost a story, delicate, clear,
Whispers of magic, drawing near.
Nature's quilt, adorned with care,
In every corner, dreams laid bare.

As the morning sun arrives,
Sparkling threads where beauty thrives.
Chasing shadows, warmth draws near,
In frosted light, the world is clear.

Embracing chill with hearts so bold,
In frosted threads, our tales are told.
Together we weave, together we stand,
In winter's grasp, hand in hand.

Patterns of Nostalgia and Chill

Whispers of seasons long gone,
Memories dance like shadows,
Flickering light at dawn,
Heartstrings pulled in meadows.

Echoes of laughter once bright,
Lingering sweet in the air,
Chasing the stars through the night,
Time paints pictures so rare.

Fragments of laughter and pain,
Carved deep in the mind's core,
Haunting like soft summer rain,
A tapestry to explore.

Each sigh a reminder of days,
Laced with the bittersweet tides,
In patterns where memory plays,
Endless where nostalgia hides.

In the Fold of Lush Warmth

Cradled in a cozy embrace,
Nature's soft blanket unspooled,
Time slows in this sacred space,
Where dreams and the heart are fueled.

Golden rays filter through trees,
Kissing the earth with their glow,
Whispers float on a soft breeze,
In harmony, all things flow.

Rustling leaves speak in soft tones,
Life flourishes all around,
In the gentle evening's moans,
Beauty in silence is found.

Wrapped in a tapestry bright,
Each thread a story to weave,
Held in the fold of pure light,
A space where we dare to believe.

Against the Icy Breath

Frost whispers secrets so stark,
A chill fills the quiet night,
Stars shiver in glimmering spark,
Hidden beneath sheets of white.

Trees bow with fragile grace,
Beneath the burden of snow,
Nature wears a shimmering lace,
Against the chill, life still flows.

Footprints trace paths on the ground,
Each step a song softly sung,
In the silence, warmth can be found,
While winter's stark bite is hung.

With courage, hearts hold their space,
Defiant against the cold breath,
In the quiet, spirits embrace,
Life dances, defying its death.

Textures of Twilight

Colors blend as daylight fades,
Soft whispers blanket the sky,
In twilight's embrace, life wades,
As stars awaken with a sigh.

Shadows stretch and mingle low,
Painting dreams on the ground,
Laughter fades with the glowing show,
In silence, new tales are found.

The cool air brushes the skin,
Inviting thoughts to take flight,
In moments where peace can begin,
As day slips gently into night.

Textures woven in hues of gray,
Nature's canvas draws us near,
In twilight's soft, wistful play,
We find the quiet we hold dear.

Milton Keynes UK
Ingram Content Group UK Ltd.
UKHW022143111124
451073UK00007B/177